PSHE AI
CITIZENSHIP

FOR AGES
9-11

Choices

Decisions

Opinions

Dilemmas

Future

Negotiations

Finding out

Planning

MOLLY POTTER

Published 2008 by A & C Black Publishers Ltd
38 Soho Square, London W1D 3HB

www.acblack.com

Dedicated to Charlie Potter

ISBN 978-0-7136-8957-0

Written by Molly Potter
Design by Cathy Tincknell
Illustration by Mike Phillips

Printed in Great Britain by Martins the Printers, Berwick-on- Tweed

This book is produced using paper that is made from wood grown in
managed, sustainable forests. It is natural, renewable and recyclable.
The logging and manufacturing processes conform to the
environmental regulations of the country of origin.

To see our full range of books visit
www.acblack.com

CONTENTS

What is PSHE and Citizenship?

Personal, Social and Health Education and Citizenship is an exciting part of the curriculum that aims to equip children and young people with the knowledge, skills, attitudes and values that will help them to make positive decisions in their lives. PSHE and Citizenship is often taught in discrete lessons but can equally well be a main feature of other lessons across the school curriculum and can be strongly connected with school ethos.

The aims of PSHE

The DCSF's framework for PSHE is non-statutory and consequently there can be some flexibility in how your school programme is structured and which areas you prioritise. This also enables your school to adjust its PSHE policy to meet the needs of your pupils in your particular setting. This book covers many learning objectives in the non-statutory PSHE curriculum and can be used to enhance any existing PSHE scheme of work. The activities can also be used to complement the SEAL curriculum and provide an alternative way of covering some of its learning objectives.

In developing your programme it might be helpful to start with the 'big picture' and consider what it is you hope to achieve with your PSHE curriculum. Your aims might include some or all of the following.
For children and young people:

- ★ To have developed a sense of self-worth and confidence.
- ★ To have developed their own individual moral framework.
- ★ To be emotionally literate – including an ability to empathise with others.
- ★ To view their future with aspiration.
- ★ To have effective communication skills, including assertiveness.
- ★ To be able to have positive relationships with others.
- ★ To have an awareness of prejudice and the harm it can cause.
- ★ To celebrate diversity and know that every individual has similar needs, rights and responsibilities.
- ★ To know how to, and be inclined to, make healthy choices.
- ★ To make informed choices.
- ★ To understand and avoid unnecessary risk of harm.
- ★ To have a discerning eye for the messages in the media.
- ★ To have an awareness and a responsibility towards local and global issues.
- ★ To know how to access help and support and how to protect themselves.

Why use this book?

Inspirational ideas: PSHE and Citizenship is full of engaging and thought provoking activities that span the information, skills, attitudes and values elements of PSHE. The activities will stimulate discussion and help pupils to explore a variety of issues through active learning, which is deemed good practice in all PSHE Guidance. Many of the activities also have cross-curricular links and need not be reserved solely for PSHE e.g. some activities lend themselves easily to writing for different purposes such as persuasive writing or journalistic writing and many activities fit very well into the current drive for 'Speaking and Listening' in schools.

How the book is organised

This book has been split into five sections:

- ★ Self-esteem and self-awareness
- ★ A focus on relationships
- ★ Exploring attitudes and values
- ★ Health and safety issues
- ★ The world around us

In the first part of each section there are teacher's notes for all of the activities. These notes outline the purpose of each activity and give key points to help you introduce concepts and guide discussions. These notes also include interesting and fun extension activities that can expand the exploration of each issue considerably. In whatever way to choose this book, whether as a focus for your school policy or as a 'dip in' resource, its fresh approach to the 'same old' learning objectives will hopefully make the delivery of PSHE more interesting for you and for your pupils!

SELF-ESTEEM AND SELF-AWARENESS

ABOUT ME (PAGE 8)

Purpose of activity:
To encourage pupils to focus on and value themselves.

Key discussion points

★ It usually feels good to be given the opportunity to share information about ourselves.

★ It's great to be able to show an interest in other people, their likes, their hobbies etc.

Extension activities

★ Pupils' sheets can be scattered around the room and each pupil could write a quiz about everyone in the class. All the answers must be somewhere on the sheets the pupils have produced.

★ All of the pupils' pages could be joined together to make a class book.

LIFE MOTTO (PAGE 9)

Purpose of activity: To reflect on outlooks and behaviours that the pupils value.

Activity notes:

Although pupils will probably want to complete the sheet individually, it's a good idea to discuss each motto as a class to check for understanding and then ask pupils to discuss further in pairs before giving a mark out of ten.

Key discussion points

★ There are a wide variety of issues covered by this activity and exploring them can be led by the discussion pupils have.

★ Some of the mottos seem more selfish than others.

★ The mottos could almost all be split into three categories:
1. mottos about keeping a healthy state of mind.
2. mottos about pushing yourself.
3. mottos about interacting with others

Extension activities

★ Pupils could illustrate the motto they consider to be most important.

★ Where pupils have given a particular motto a low score, they could explore whether they would value a motto with the converse meaning.

★ Pupils could take the sheet home and ask their parents/carers to complete the activity.

★ Pupils could try and turn their life philosophy into a metaphor, saying or story.

A MANUAL FOR ME! (PAGE 10)

Purpose of activity: To explore preferences and dislikes – in an imaginative way.

Key discussion points

★ We all have different personal preferences and this activity will highlight this. Pupils can share and discuss their personal choices and their reasons for choosing each thing. Some pupils may change their minds when they hear other people's reasons for choosing each thing.

Extension activities

★ Pupils could 'draw' a few photographs of themselves on Nozor.

★ Pupils could draw and write a postcard from Nozor.

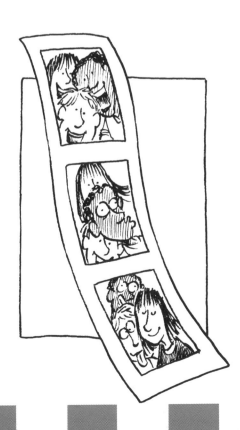

AN IDEAL TIME LINE (PAGE 11)

Purpose of activity: For pupils to consider their future and start to develop aspirations.

Key discussion points

★ The timings of major events in people's lives vary – sometimes because of conscious decisions and sometimes because of things beyond a person's control. Pupils can consider the life choices that they believe would be beneficial to a person.

★ In sharing their timelines, many issues about what to do and when to do them will arise.

Extension activities

★ Discuss the benefits and disadvantages of having children at a younger or an older age.

★ Discuss the different types of education a person can go on to after leaving school e.g. vocational training, further education, higher education.

WISHES FOR YOUR FUTURE (PAGE 12)

Purpose of activity: For pupils to explore their future with aspiration and to consider what their parents/carers might want for their future.

Key discussion points

★ Most adults did not consider their future when they were a child.

★ Some people find it helpful to have aspirations and dreams.

★ Sometimes, people assume that they will do

exactly the same as their parents/carers have done.

Extension activities

★ Pupils could draw a time line and discuss what they would ideally like to be doing at different ages through out their lives.

★ Pupils can consider the changes that they think they will witness in their lifetime.

★ Pupils could take this sheet home and discuss the ideas with their parents/carers.

YOU AS AN ADULT (PAGE 13)

Purpose of activity: To develop ideas about their individual futures.

Key discussion issues

★ Obviously nobody can predict the future but speculating about it can beneficially influence decisions a person might make.

Extension activities

★ Pupils could draw themselves at age 25 and list as many details about themselves as they can speculate about.

★ Pupils could make 'I predict' booklets to keep. In it they can include not only details that they predict about themselves but also things they think will be invented in their lifetimes, what their house will look like, how fashion will change, how travel will change etc.

OPTIMIST OR PESSIMIST? (PAGE 14)

Purpose of activity: to consider how most situations can be looked at both positively or negatively and how the former usually makes people more resilient.

Key discussion points

★ The same person can be both optimistic and pessimistic in different situations but people can also have a tendency towards being either optimistic or pessimistic.

★ Pessimism can be destructive and stop problems from getting solved.

★ Optimistic people are more likely to enjoy life

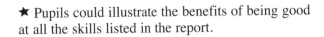

and get more out of it.

Extension activities

★ Pupils could try and make up some proverbs about optimists and pessimists.

★ Pupils could draw Pat Pessimist and Olive/r Optimist cartoons showing how they deal with different situations.

★ Pupils could consider the story of two identical cities with two men leaving each city to go to the other. The two men bump into each other halfway between the two cities and ask each other what the city they are travelling to is like. One says, 'It's full of beggars and thieves,' but the other says, 'the city I just left is full of happy and kind people.' Both men travel on and are surprised to find a city full of not what the man they met said, but of the same things that were in the city they just left. We see what we go looking for!

SKILLS FOR LIFE (PAGE 15)

Purpose of activity: To self reflect.

Key discussion points

★ Pupils might need help in understanding some of the skills.

★ All the skills on the report sheet are generally considered to be positive qualities.

Extension activites

★ Pupils could fill in a report card for a friend.

★ Pupils could think of other life skills that could have been included in the report.

★ Pupils could illustrate the benefits of being good at all the skills listed in the report.

HOW DO I BEHAVE AT SCHOOL? (PAGE 16)

Purpose of activity: For pupils to reflect on their behaviour at school.

Key discussion points

★ In an ideal world, everyone would have their own moral code that would help them to do well and would make them considerate and respectful towards others. Some people take longer to develop this than others for a variety of reasons.

★ If a pupil is at risk from harm, an adult needs to be told. If a pupil is just doing something silly or naughty that will cause no harm, it can be a good idea for a pupil to try to persuade them to stop. Always telling the teacher about other pupils' misbehaviour can make someone very unpopular.

Extension activities

★ Pupils could discuss why they think some children misbehave in school.

★ Pupils could consider the moral dilemmas in questions 3, 4, 5 or 6 and illustrate all possible outcomes. They could then write what they think about each outcome (what makes it the wrong/right thing to do and why someone might choose to do this).

ABOUT ME

You are going to fill up two sides of A3 paper with lots of information about yourself so that someone can see at a glance what sort of person your are. Start by drawing a large cartoon picture of yourself in the middle of one side of the paper.

Here are some ideas to help you:

★ List three things that make you:
a) excited b) scared c) happy d) angry or irritated

★ What do you do in your spare time? Have you got any hobbies? Do you play a musical instrument? What do you find relaxing? Do you have any pets?

★ Ask a few people in your class to choose three of the following words that they think could be used to describe you:

    kind, helpful, funny, a good listener, cheerful, interesting, good company, patient, creative.

Draw a graph to show what you find.

★ Draw a map of your neighbourhood. Label all the places you like to visit.

★ List your favourite and your least favourite from each of the following categories:

    colour, animal, insect, chocolate bar, fruit, flavour of crisps, vegetable, sport, drink, **TV** programme, lesson, bird, shape, weather, season, day, shop, thing to do.

★ Draw a plan of your bedroom and label the things that are special to you.

★ Draw a picture of yourself wearing an outfit you would love to have made for you.

★ List and draw five people that are special to you.

★ Write about what would happen on your most perfect day.

★ Draw some speech bubbles and write some nice things people have said about you inside them. If you can't remember any, ask a couple of friends to say something nice about you and write down their comments.

> You're a really good mate.

★ When you grow up:
    What job do you want? Where do you want to live? Will you be rich? Will you get married? Will you have children? What will your house be like? What will your hobbies be? What will your friends be like?

★ Is there anything you have strong opinions about? Like being a vegetarian, animal rights, people's rights, prejudice, the environment?

★ Draw a time line of your life so far.

★ What if...
    you could receive any five gifts tomorrow, what would they be?
    you could change your name, what would it be?
    you could wake up tomorrow with a skill you don't have today, what would it be?
    you were an animal, what would you be?

A life philosophy (i.e. what you believe about life) can be written as a motto – a few words that sum up what you believe.

For each of the following mottos, give a mark out of ten for how important you think it would be in explaining how you plan to live your life.

MOTTO	MARK 10–spot on 0–not at all
Live life to the full – do as much as you can	
Find as many opportunities as possible to learn	
Treat others as you would expect to be treated yourself	
Have as much fun and enjoyment as possible	
Achieve lots and often – be a winner!	
Make people notice you – stand out from the crowd	
Love well and lots – friends, partners and relatives	
Treat yourself kindly – never be too hard on yourself	
Forgive and move on – never hold grudges	
Look to the future with aspiration	
Work is important	
Have a positive outlook – look for good in everything	
Learn from your mistakes	
Take as much as you can get	
Forgive yourself for your failures and weaknesses	
You are the most important person – no one else will believe that for you	
Never take anything too seriously	
Regret is pointless	
Never make assumptions about other people	
Owning nice things makes life sweeter	
It's good to keep busy	
Friendships are really important	
Variety and change make life interesting	
Worrying is a waste of time	

IF THERE IS TIME...

If you had to choose one of the above mottos that you think you could value for the rest of your life, which would it be? If you need to make another one up, do so!

PSHE AND CITIZENSHIP 9-11 © MOLLY POTTER 2008

A MANUAL FOR ME!

The island of Nozor is a very special place and people love to go there on holiday. When people get to Nozor, they can't believe their luck because they become the centre of attention and everything is magically tailored to their needs.

The creatures on the island are called Kalar. They try incredibly hard to keep their guests happy by following the manual that each person provides before they arrive in Nozor. This manual includes all the details about how a person would and would not like to be treated.

You are going to spend three days on Nozor and therefore need to write the manual that will tell the Kalar how to treat you. All your basic needs (water, food, showers etc) will be met but if you don't write what else you would like, then it won't happen! You also need to be clear about things you definitely don't want to happen because the Kalar sometimes surprise people with things they didn't write about.

SECTION	EXAMPLES OF THINGS PEOPLE HAVE INCLUDED IN THE PAST
Food	I will need to eat buttered toast once a day. I would like a bowl of fresh fruit salad near me at all times. I want sausages for breakfast every day. Never attempt to give me brussel sprouts. On the first day I want roast chicken, on the second day, pizza, etc.
Entertainment	I want to have a castle with lots of secret passages to explore. I want to play rounders twice in the three days. I want to have huge bits of paper and lots of paints to make pictures with. I want my own bumper cars to play in all the time.
Things I like to talk about	My friends and what they have been up to. The solar system.
People I like to spend time with	I want my mum there all the time. I want my friend George to visit me for two hours on the second day. I want a different friend to play with each evening. Jan on Monday...
Morning routine	Every morning I want to be woken up at 6 a.m. by being tickled. I want breakfast in bed. I want someone to comb my hair for ten minutes every morning.
Where you sleep	I want a huge bed. I want to sleep on a furry rug. I want to sleep in a hammock.
Things I need to be kept away from me	Spiders Homework The smell of rubbish People who shout
Dos	Call me by my first name: Gerald Give me a massage once a day. Smile at me and give me compliments.
Don'ts	Make me have to concentrate. Tell me off. Look over my shoulder at what I'm doing.
The view from my bedroom window	Swirling colours Make this different every day People walking by – so it's interesting to watch

If you were to map out a person's life, at what age do you think it would be best to do each of the following things? Mark them on this time path. For some of these your answer might be 'never'.

- ★ Start to have children
- ★ Buy a house
- ★ Be fit and healthy until
- ★ Die
- ★ Find a partner that they will be with for the rest of their life

- ★ Learn to drive
- ★ Get their first full time job
- ★ Leave school
- ★ Have grandchildren
- ★ Move away from home

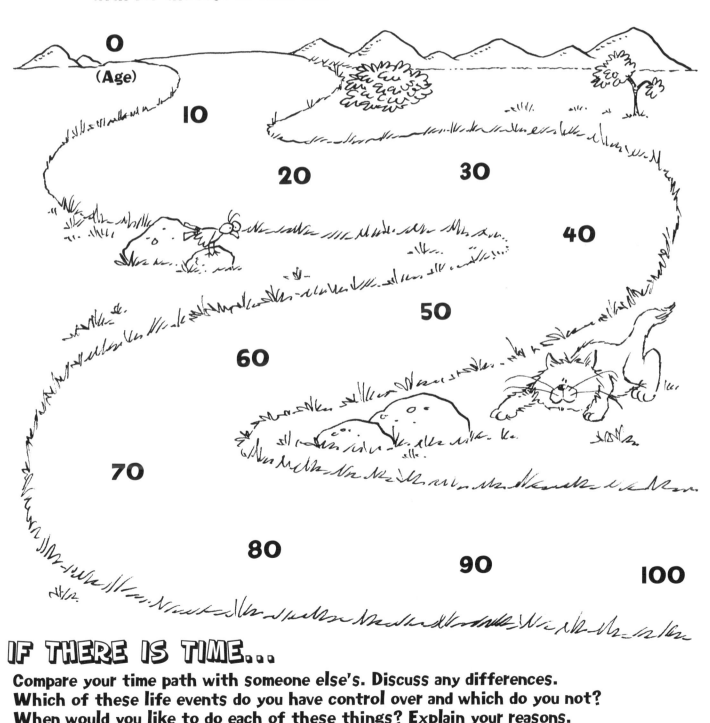

PSHE AND CITIZENSHIP 9-11 © MOLLY POTTER 2008

IF THERE IS TIME...

Compare your time path with someone else's. Discuss any differences.
Which of these life events do you have control over and which do you not?
When would you like to do each of these things? Explain your reasons.

WISHES FOR YOUR FUTURE

Complete this form as honestly as you can..

Will you...	How much would you like to do this? Give a mark out of 10. (0 means not at all. 10 means you really want to.)	How much do you think your parents or carers would like you to do this? Give a mark out of 10. (0 means not at all. 10 means they really want you to.)	Any comments
be sensible with money?			
learn to drive?			
go to university or college?			
have children before you are twenty?			
get a well paid job?			
get a job you really enjoy?			
find a partner for life that you are happy with?			
have children?			
get married?			
have lots of friends?			
find things you really enjoy doing?			
grow up to be a kind person?			
travel to other places in Britain?			
own your own home?			
travel and see other countries?			
not smoke?			
be fit and healthy?			
live near your family?			
never break the law?			

IF THERE IS TIME...

★ Do you have any other hopes and dreams for your life?
★ If you could make one wish for your future that would definitely happen, what would it be?

PSHE AND CITIZENSHIP 9-11 © MOLLY POTTER 2008

WHAT KIND OF ADULT DO YOU THINK YOU WILL BE?

Discuss the following with a partner.

VALUES AND PERSONALITY

Do you think...
* ★ having lots of money will be important to you?
* ★ having a job that you really enjoy will be important to you?
* ★ being happy will be important to you. What do you think will keep you happy?
* ★ you will ever break the law?
* ★ you will do things that you are proud of?
* ★ you will find some things difficult and if so, what?

Do you think you will be...
* ★ a person who needs lots of adventure and excitement in life?
* ★ a person who loves to be with your children (if you have them)?
* ★ a confident person?
* ★ willing to help other people?
* ★ a worrier?
* ★ a very active person, a lazy person or somewhere in between?
* ★ an optimist or a pessimist?
* ★ an honest person?
* ★ someone who wants to be like everyone else or be unusual?

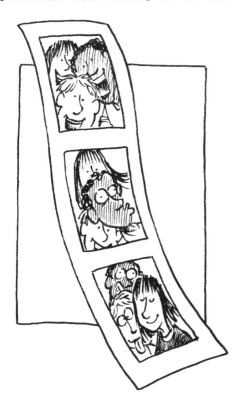

FRIENDS AND SOCIAL LIFE
* ★ Do you think you will have lots of friends or a small number of close friends?
* ★ What kind of things do you think you will do with your friends? (e.g. go to the pub, go to parties, have dinner parties at each others' houses, go to the cinema, do hobbies together)
* ★ What do you think your friends will be like?
* ★ What do you think your friends will like about you?

FREE TIME
* ★ Do you think you will have hobbies?
* ★ Will you watch lots of television?
* ★ Do you think you will be a person who loves being at home?
* ★ Will you exercise and if so, how?
* ★ Do you think you will go travelling?
* ★ How do you think you will spend most of your free time?

AMBITIONS AND ACHIEVEMENTS
* ★ What ambitions will you have as an adult?
* ★ What do you think you will achieve?
* ★ Can you think of anything you definitely don't want to do?

PSHE AND CITIZENSHIP 9-11 © MOLLY POTTER 2008

OPTIMIST OR PESSIMIST?

An **OPTIMIST** tends to look at the positive or good in any situation.

A PESSIMIST tends to look at the negative or bad in any situation.

An optimist would say that this glass is half full but a pessimist would say that this glass is half empty.

1. Can you see how the idea of a glass being half full or half empty helps to explain how an optimist is different from a pessimist?

2. Sort the following into things a pessimist tends to do and things an optimist tends to do.

	Optimist or pessimist?		Optimist or pessimist?
criticises others		makes the best of a bad situation	
is cheerful		sees mistakes as an opportunity to learn	
moans about things a lot		gives up easily if things don't go to plan	
sees people as having different strengths		is angry or miserable when they make mistakes	
is enthusiastic		is miserable	

3. Do you consider yourself to be more of an optimist (positive thinker) or a pessimist (negative thinker)?

4. Imagine you were stuck in a slow moving queue. What might an optimist think and do and what might a pessimist think and do?

IF THERE IS TIME...

Role-play Pat Pessimist and Oliver Optimist trying really hard to solve a maths problem. Feel free to exaggerate!

PSHE AND CITIZENSHIP 9-11 © MOLLY POTTER 2008

SKILLS FOR LIFE

Work with a partner.
For each life skill in the table:
   a) discuss what it means
   b) think of an example of the skill in action

Now write your own report. Grade yourself for how good you think you are at each skill and write a comment.

A very good	B good	C middling	D poor	E very poor

REPORT CARD FOR ....

SKILL	GRADE	COMMENT
FORGIVING PEOPLE THAT HAVE UPSET YOU		
BEING TACTFUL		
EXPLAINING HOW YOU FEEL		
BEING ASSERTIVE		
COMPROMISING		
LISTENING		
GIVING COMPLIMENTS		
BEING DETERMINED		
ASKING FOR HELP IF YOU NEED IT		
POSITIVE THINKING		

PSHE AND CITIZENSHIP 9-11 © MOLLY POTTER 2008

Try and answer these questions as honestly as you can.

1) If I don't understand something in a lesson straight away:

☐ A) I keep trying very hard to see if I can understand it and keep asking for help until I do.

☐ B) I wait until someone notices that I haven't understood.

☐ C) I don't try very hard and just hope I can get away with not having to do it.

☐ D) I just give up and mess around.

2) If someone is messing around in class:

☐ A) I try to persuade them kindly, not to mess around.

☐ B) I ignore them.

☐ C) I laugh at them.

☐ D) I join in and start messing around too.

3) If I accidentally broke a piece of school equipment, I would:

☐ A) own up to it.

☐ B) just put it back where I found it.

☐ C) hide it.

☐ D) blame someone else.

4) At playtime, if I saw a person upset because they were being teased by a friend of mine, I would:

☐ A) go and try and stop the teasing.

☐ B) go and tell an adult.

☐ C) not do anything.

☐ D) join in and tease the person.

5) If I saw someone copying in a test, I would:

☐ A) try to persuade the person not to copy.

☐ B) tell the teacher.

☐ C) do nothing.

☐ D) try and copy too.

6) If I found a £5 note on the floor in the corridor, I would:

☐ A) take it into class and hand it over to the teacher.

☐ B) ask my friends if it belonged to them.

☐ C) check that no one I knew had lost any money and if they hadn't, I would keep it.

☐ D) put it in my pocket and keep it.

7) I am aware of school rules and I break them:

☐ A) hardly ever or not at all.

☐ B) occasionally.

☐ C) often.

☐ D) all the time.

8) At school, I do what I am meant to be doing:

☐ A) all the time

☐ B) most of the time

☐ C) occasionally

☐ D) hardly ever

Mostly 'A's
You are a star!

Mostly 'B's
You are probably a pleasant person to have in school.

Mostly 'C's
You might need to put some effort into improving your behaviour.

Mostly 'D's
Ask yourself why you behave like this and see if you can improve, one step at a time.

A FOCUS ON RELATIONSHIPS

MY FRIENDS (PAGE 20)

Purpose of the activity: To consider the varied roles friends play.

Key discussion points

★ Although many people consider themselves to have a best friend, in reality different friendships fulfil many different roles.

★ A good friend is a very valuable things.

★ Friends do sometimes make mistakes and let us down and we can't expect anyone to be perfect. Forgiveness is an important part of friendships.

Extension activities

★ Pupils could make their friends feel good by telling them that they put their name into the table.

★ Pupils could write several sentence completions for, 'My friends are great because.'

★ Pupils could write a friendships problem page. One pupil could write the question and another could write the advice.

THE DOS AND DON'TS OF A FRIENDSHIP (PAGE 21)

Purpose of this activity: For pupils to consider behaviour that can damage and behaviour that can strengthen a friendship

Key discussion points

★ Friends can do things without realising that they have upset you.

★ Many friendships can suffer for a while because of something a person has done. It is nearly always best to communicate with a friend directly and assertively if they upset you, so they are given an opportunity to apologise and clear the air.

Extension activities

★ Pupils can consider a time when a friend did something kind for them.

★ Pupils can consider a particular friendship and what it gives them.

★ Pupils can discuss the idea of having different friends for different things e.g. a friend that you ask to talk something through with you might not be the friend that you would go to to have a laugh.

TEAMWORK (PAGE 22)

Purpose of this activity: For pupils to consider what makes a team work well together.

Key discussion points

★ Some people find teamwork really difficult.

★ A good team member:

1. Shares ideas and makes suggestions without assuming everyone will just do what has been suggested.
2. Does not get angry or upset if everyone agrees to do something that they did not suggest.
3. Listens well to suggestions and discusses each one – searching for improvements.
4. Speaks politely and calmly and aims to have only one person speaking at a time.
5. Cooperates when it has been decided what is going to be done.
6. Keeps the goal clear in their head and keeps focussed on the task.
7. Shares the responsibilities of completing the task.

★ In some teams, one person can emerge as the 'leader' – this can work well as long as there is not a conflict over who this should be and as long as the leader listens to the suggestions everyone makes.

Extension activities

★ You could set pupils another task (e.g. build the highest tower using sticky tape and newspaper) and tell pupils that you are going to deliberately plant teamwork 'saboteurs' in different groups. Ask pupils to guess how the saboteur was behaving and discuss his/her impact. Behaviour instructions to the saboteur could include:

1. Be bossy
2. Do nothing unless you are told to
3. Just do your own thing
4. Argue with every suggestions
5. Don't listen
6. Never do what you are asked to do
7. Keep talking about things that are nothing to do with the task

★ Pupils could write 'A Guide to Teamwork' leaflet.

★ Pupils could imagine a school where none of the adults in it worked as a team and discuss what would happen.

SAM MADE PAT ANGRY (PAGE 23)

Purpose of the activity: To look at different ways of responding to someone making you angry and to know what assertiveness is.

Key discussion points

★ Assertiveness does not always work but it has more chance of working than the other three responses.

★ Assertiveness can save time and clear the air more quickly than any of the other responses.

★ If people respond passively, they are likely to remain angry and end up feeling angry with themselves.

★ If people respond aggressively, the situation can sometimes escalate or the person who has made them angry enjoys the fact they got such a strong response.

★ Responding indirectly can include ignoring the person, gossiping about them, trying to make other people moan about them etc. This can mean the bad feeling can hang around for some time as it never really makes the upset person feel better about the situation.

★ If someone has upset you, it is best to deal directly with the person. A one to one talk where both people listen to each other and apologise – if necessary – can clear the air and everyone will feel much better!

★ An assertive comment can include a statement about how what happened made the person feel – especially if it is a friend who caused the upset e.g. I felt really upset when…

★ Traditionally, females are considered to respond passively and indirectly and males to respond aggressively. This could be discussed.

Extension activities

★ Pupils could make 'Be Assertive' posters.

★ Pupils could explore assertive and non assertive body language. They could try out the following and decide whether it makes a person assertive or not: giving eye contact/looking at the ground, standing tall/hunching, speaking in a quiet voice/speaking in a firm and friendly tone, staying calm/getting agitated.

GOOD COMMUNICATION (PAGE 24)

Purpose of this activity: For pupils to consider different ways of communicating and those which help and those which hinder relationships.

Key discussion points

Ensure pupils understand all the communication terminology. It is helpful to give examples of each type.

★ Effective communication can sort out many difficulties and problems in situations and relationships.

★ Some forms of communication can make other people feel angry, irritated or not valued.

★ When communication breaks down, resentment can build up and people can remain angry or upset.

Extension activities

★ Pupils could role-play a negotiation in pairs where:

1. One child wants to join in with a game of football and the other wants to continue playing Frisbee.

2. One child wants to go to the cinema and the other wants to go shopping.

★ Pupils could draw cartoon pictures that illustrate positive and negative communication.

★ Pupils could develop some dialogue and body language for the following characters: Bossy Brian, Critical Clive, Judging Judy, Patronising Penelope and Moaning Maud.

EFFECTIVE COMMUNICATION (PAGE 25)

Purpose of activity: To consider positive communication.

Key discussion points

★ It is easy to 'mess up' when it comes to communication. When things are 'messed up' further communication is usually needed to sort it out.

Extension activities

★ Pupils could choose one of the scenarios to role-play and then redo the same scene but with positive communication.

★ Pupils could write letters of advice to the characters in the table.

★ Pupils could act out a public information film about good communication skills!

CRITICISE OR SUGGEST? (PAGE 26)

Purpose of activity: To consider the impact of criticising in contrast to making suggestions.

Key discussion points

★ No one likes to receive criticism although some people can cope with it better than others because of good self-esteem.

★ Most criticisms can be changed to sound like suggestions and this is sometimes termed: constructive criticism.

★ Criticising is easy to do because all you have to do is say something negative about what has been produced. Making suggestions is more difficult because you have to actually think of improvements that could be made.

★ Sometimes people criticise something that a person could never change (e.g. their physical appearance), how someone does something that they cannot change (e.g. how they walk) or a personal choice (e.g. a new coat they have bought). This is only ever unkind.

Extension activities

★ Pupils could explore the notion that if you cannot make a suggestion as to how something could be improved, then it is only kind to say something positive. Pupils could try and make up a proverb that imparts this advice e.g. if you can't do better, it's worth praise.

★ Pupils could explore how the tone of voice makes a difference to how feedback is made through role-playing the answers they have made up in the activity.

INVESTIGATING SIMILARITIES AND DIFFERENCES (PAGE 27)

Purpose of the activity: To appreciate that people have similarities and differences and to prompt discussions where pupils show an interest in each other.

Key discussion points

★ There are many similarities common to all.

★ Basic needs – that all humans share – are often considered to be rights.

★ No two people are the same, as humans can be different in a variety of ways – physically, with preferences, with attitudes, opinions and values, with lifestyle and with abilities.

★ When people show an interest in us, it can make us feel good.

Extension activities

★ Once pupils have composed their lists, they can form groups of four and share ideas for finding more similarities and more differences.

★ Pupils could try and do the same activity but in threes – where they find similarities (for all three and differences (for all three). This is, of course, more difficult.

★ Pupils could make up slogans and/or adverts that help people to celebrate difference and diversity.

WHAT ASSUMPTIONS DO WE MAKE? (PAGE 28)

Purpose of the activity: To explore prejudices and the assumptions and look at how these can rarely be helpful.

Key discussion points:

★ We all have prejudices that lead us to make assumptions about people based on what people look like or small pieces of information we have about them.

★ We could try to be aware of our prejudices so that we can challenge them in ourselves.

★ If we do make assumptions about people, we must try not to let them affect how we greet people or let conversations develop.

★ It is best to try to treat everyone as an individual and not make any assumptions.

★ How can we encourage people to celebrate diversity of every kind and help people see that the world would be a very dull place if we were all the same?

★ Do people fear things that are different and if so, why?

Extension activities

★ Pupils could explore the reasons why a person might be treated badly because they are different in some way. They could make up a cartoon or story about a person or creature being excluded for being different and how this eventually meant that everyone missed out.

★ Pupils could make up a story based on the saying, 'never judge a book by its cover'.

MY FRIENDS

See how many different people you can put on to this sheet.

A friend you would turn to if you were upset.

A friend you find interesting to talk to.

A friend you would take shopping with you.

A friend you feel comfortable being with.

A friend you would spend time with to have fun.

A friend you know likes to do similar things to you.

A friend you really enjoy spending time with.

A friend that makes you feel good about yourself.

A friend you would turn to if someone was teasing you.

A friend you would turn to if you needed some ideas for a project.

A friend that you completely trust.

A person you would like to get to know a bit better.

A friend that you can trust to treat you the same each time you get together.

A friend that challenges you.

CAN YOU ADD ANY MORE?

PSHE AND CITIZENSHIP 9-11 © MOLLY POTTER 2008

THE DOS AND DON'TS OF A FRIENDSHIP

Here are some complaints people made about their friends.

"Quite often I tell Sam about something I did and he judges me and makes me feel bad."

"I have a friend who I know talks about me behind my back every time we have had a little argument."

"If I tell Leah about something that is upsetting me she makes out like I am making a big fuss over nothing."

"I have a friend that is always arranging to do things with me but then more often than not cancels it."

"My friend always insists that we do exactly what s/he wants to do."

"Joss teases me and laughs at me whenever we are with other people but is really nice to me when we are alone."

1. Take each statement and discuss how the friend is damaging the friendship.
2. Do you think any of your friends would ever say any of these things about you?
3. Award a mark out of 10 for how important you consider the following things to be in a friendship.

I think that when you are friends with people it is important...	Mark out of 10. (10 means it's really important)
...that you don't judge them.	
...that you take their worries seriously.	
...that you don't tease them.	
...that you try to be reliable and keep to any commitments or plans you make.	
...that you don't talk about them behind their back.	
...that you listen to them if they need to talk about something.	
...that you make time to be with them.	
...that you stick up for them.	
...that you don't pressurise them into doing things they don't really want to do.	
...that you like what is unique about them.	
...that you forgive them if they do something that upsets you.	
...you make efforts to talk things through if the friendship has any problems.	
...you compromise when you want to do different things.	
NOW ADD TWO OF YOUR OWN	

PSHE AND CITIZENSHIP 9-11 © MOLLY POTTER 2008

TEAMWORK

In a team of four or five, work together to do the following tasks.

Make up a name for a new chocolate and mint flavoured, stripy toothpaste. It needs to be a name that people will remember and that helps people remember what is special about the toothpaste.

If you had to make things for a person that was 10cm tall, list what you would use to make the following:
* ★ a chair
* ★ a table
* ★ a cup
* ★ a comfortable bed
* ★ a type of transport that would mean he or she could move faster than walking pace

Draw a picture of each thing and label what it is made of.

Take a piece of scrap paper and try to tear a perfect circle shape out of it. You have to tear the circle (no scissors, knives or sharp points to cut the paper) but you can use anything else you can find in the room. You are allowed more than one attempt at this but don't expect your circle to be perfect!

Think of the best idea you can to entertain a 6 year old child for 15 minutes with just a ping pong ball in a playground!

Work out a secret signal that could be used to 'point' at different objects in the room so that everyone in the team knows which object you are pointing to. The signal needs to be secret enough so that anyone not in your team doesn't know what you were pointing to.

Now consider how well your team worked together by asking the following questions:

	Yes	No
Did everyone join in with the task?		
Did people listen well to each other?		
Were lots of suggestions made about how to complete the task and were they thought through properly?		
Did anyone seem to be in charge?		
Did anyone get angry?		
Was anyone bossy without listening to what anyone else had to say?		
Did everyone get a chance to make suggestions?		
Was every suggestion discussed?		
Did anyone just get on with the task without asking or explaining to anyone else?		
Overall, do you think your team worked well together?		

IF THERE IS TIME...

★ Decide which task your team worked together best at. How did people behave in that task?

★ Discuss what you think makes a team of people work well together?

PSHE AND CITIZENSHIP 9-11 © MOLLY POTTER 2008

SAM MADE PAT ANGRY!

Sam and Pat are friends. However, one Monday morning Sam insulted Pat in front of everyone in the playground. Everyone laughed.

Look at the different responses Pat could have:

PASSIVE

Pat just took the teasing and did nothing about it even though it was upsetting.

AGGRESSIVE

Pat shoved Sam and said that Sam was 'useless' and 'a rubbish friend'.

INDIRECT

Pat just took the teasing, but later on spent ages moaning about Sam to Ashley (behind Sam's back) and refused to talk to Sam from that time onwards.

ASSERTIVE

Pat said clearly to Sam, 'I don't need your insults, what are you trying to do? I think you need to say sorry to me for that if you think our friendship is worth anything.'

DISCUSS THESE QUESTIONS

1. Which of the four ways do you think was the best way of dealing with the insult?
2. If the insult made Pat angry, how do you think Pat would feel after each of the four responses?
3. How might Sam feel after each of the responses?
4. What advice would you give to Pat and Sam to help them be good friends again?
5. If someone is assertive, they say what they want to happen without making the other person feel upset or angry. What would be an assertive response to the following situations?

a) Katie tries to persuade Yuri to go and steal a chocolate bar out of Sandy's lunchbox.

b) Jon tries to persuade Poppy to let him copy all her homework.

c) Gina laughs at Josie's painting and says that it looks awful.

PSHE AND CITIZENSHIP 9-11 © MOLLY POTTER 2008

GOOD COMMUNICATION

GOOD COMMUNICATION	POOR COMMUNICATION
Negotiating – exchanging ideas, information, and opinions with others to arrive jointly at decisions, conclusions, or solutions.	Not being prepared to talk about any changes to what you want.
Compromising – giving up part of what you want so that you arrive at a solution that you are all happy with.	Always insisting on doing exactly what you want.
Being assertive – being up front and clear about what you want without upsetting the person you are talking to.	Being aggressive, passive (giving in) gossiping or moaning behind someone's back.
Being sympathetic and having empathy –being supportive of a person's worries or concerns and trying to understand how they must be feeling.	Not listening when someone is upset, making out their concern is no big deal, hogging the conversation with your own problems or joking when they want to be serious.
Expressing how you feel – explaining how you feel.	Bottling up how you feel.
Making suggestions and commenting politely – suggesting improvements and avoiding negative remarks.	Criticising, bossing, judging, patronising, etc.
Listening well – paying attention, giving eye contact, not being distracted and letting other people finish their sentences.	Not listening, talking over people or not letting a person finish what they are saying.
Discussing solutions and praising – concentrating on the possibilities and positive things rather than the difficulties and problems.	Blaming others, moaning, always pointing out bad things.

Sports day is boring.

I. Read through the two different types of communication in the table above and decide which type of communication the following are:

★ "That was Jamie's fault – stupid boy – he left that there"
★ "I feel really upset. Can we talk about it please?"
★ "I'm going on that day and that's final, I don't care if it makes things difficult for you."
★ "You poor thing, that must have been terrible for you. How do you feel now?"
★ "I think his painting is rubbish."

★ "No, I don't want to go to your stupid party."
★ "O.K. How about we do what you want today and what I want tomorrow."
★ "Go over there and get out of the way."
★ "That's absolutely brilliant – well done"
★ "You could make that title a bit bigger. That would make it look even better."
★ "Sports day is boring. I never win and I don't like sport or being outside."

That's absolutely brilliant– well done!

IF THERE IS TIME...
Consider some of the things you have said to people in the last day or so. Can you think of an example of 'good' communication or 'poor' communication'?

EFFECTIVE COMMUNICATION

SCENARIOS

SCENARIO A
Greg was quite clearly upset about something that had happened at home that morning. However, his mate Jake just laughed at him and told him not to be so stupid.

SCENARIO B
Sari and Ashley are good friends. However, this week Sari annoyed Ashley because she went to the cinema with another friend even though Sari had said they would go together. Ashley has started moaning about Sari to other people behind her back and ignoring her whenever she is around.

SCENARIO C
Farida wanted to go and meet some other friends in town but Henry didn't feel like it. They argued about what they were going to do and in the end Farida stormed off to town, leaving Henry on his own.

SCENARIO D
James persuaded Charlie to let him copy his homework, even though it would be obvious that this had happened and they would probably both get into trouble for it.

SCENARIO E
Ali had just painted a picture that he felt reasonably proud of. Ali asked Harry for his opinion and if he thought the picture could be improved. Harry just criticised everything, leaving Ali feeling angry and no longer interested in his painting.

It would have been better if they had...
* ★ been assertive
* ★ made suggestions and been complimentary
* ★ listened, been supportive and sympathetic
* ★ moaned behind their friend's back and sulked
* ★ laughed inappropriately
* ★ criticised
* ★ expressed their feelings openly
* ★ negotiated and compromised
* ★ disagreed
* ★ given in

Complete the table below about the scenarios A to E using the list above to help you.

	What she/he did	It would have been better if she/he had...
Jake		
Ashley		
Farida and Henry		
Charlie		
Harry		

IF THERE IS TIME...

Discuss with a partner. Why, when it seems obvious that 'good' communication helps everyone feel better, do people not always communicate positively?

PSHE AND CITIZENSHIP 9-11 © MOLLY POTTER 2008

CRITICISE OR SUGGEST?

To criticise means to point out what is wrong with something or someone.
To suggest means to give an idea.

Jonty painted a picture and he was quite pleased with it. He asked Joss what she thought of his picture and she said:

"It's rather messy and I don't like the colours you have used."

He then asked Frankie what he thought of the picture and he said:

"I think you could paint a straight line to make that edge a bit neater and I think it would look even better if you painted that plain bit yellow — what do you think?"

1. Which of the comments do you think is a suggestion and which do you think is a criticism?
2. Which comment would you rather someone said to you?
3. It's easier to criticise than make a suggestion, why do you think that is?
4. Write a criticism for each of the following. Then write a suggestion that could be used instead of the criticism.

Pedro shows you a poster he has made to advertise the school fete. The writing is not very clear.

Zara shows you a vegetable pet that she is going to enter into a competition. The legs look like they have been stuck in the wrong places and this means the model keeps falling over.

Criticism	Criticism
Suggestion	Suggestion

SIMILARITIES AND DIFFERENCES

Work with a partner. You are going to try and develop the longest lists you can. The table shows you what will be in each of your lists. For every difference you find you need to find a similarity. You must therefore end up with the same number of both.

SIMILARITIES – all the things you can think of that are similar or the same about you and your partner.	DIFFERENCES – all the things you can think of that are different about you and your partner.

Here are some prompts and examples to help you.

PHYSICAL (WHAT YOU CAN DO AND WHAT YOU LOOK LIKE)
You both breathe, what else do you both do?
What about hair colour, skin colour and eye colour, are they the same or different?
Can you both roll your tongue?
How far can you jump from standing?
Are you left or right handed?
What else?

PREFERENCES (WHAT YOU LIKE AND DON'T LIKE)
What are your favourite colours?
Which lesson do you like best at school?
What are your favourite animals?
Would you rather ride a bike or walk?
Would you rather read a book or paint a picture?
What else?

HOW YOU LIVE
What time do you eat your dinner?
What time do you go to bed?
How do you travel to school?
Do you have a bedroom of your own?
What chores do you have to do at home?

YOUR OPINIONS, BELIEFS AND THOUGHTS
Do you believe in ghosts?
Are you a vegetarian?
What do you like best about school?
What do you think is most important for a person's happiness?

AND ANY OTHERS YOU CAN FIND...
What colour is your toothbrush?
How many brothers or sisters do you have?
What are you good at?

PSHE AND CITIZENSHIP 9-11 © MOLLY POTTER 2008

WHAT ASSUMPTIONS DO WE MAKE?

An assumption is where we come to a decision about a person before we actually know if it's true or not e.g. you might assume that a scruffy person is lazy. This is not a good thing to assume.

Everyone makes assumptions. Sometimes we make assumptions about people so that we don't have to bother finding things out. Sometimes assumptions can make us judge a person before we know them properly.

1. If you had to choose on looks alone, which of the following would you most like and least like to be...
   a) your doctor?
   b) knocking on your front door to ask you something?
   c) a neighbour?
   d) your teacher?

Discuss with a partner: What were the reasons for choosing the people you did? What assumptions did you make based on what they looked like?

2. Draw a picture of what you would expect a head teacher to look like. Now draw a picture of a person that you would never expect to be a head teacher. Look at your two pictures. What assumptions have you made?

3. Consider honestly what thoughts and feelings you have when you think about the following types of people:
   ★ A scruffy person
   ★ A very clever person
   ★ An old person
   ★ A polite person
   ★ A person shouting at another person
   ★ A parent
   ★ A person in a wheelchair

Would you make any assumptions about any of the types of people above? If you have, how could you be sure that your assumptions were true?

IF THERE IS TIME...

What advice would you give to people about making assumptions? Make a poster that clearly gives this advice. Here are some ideas to help you:
   ★ If you assume things about people, you can end up judging them before you know them.
   ★ Expect everyone to be different.
   ★ Get to know everyone individually.
   ★ Most people don't like having assumptions made about them.

PSHE AND CITIZENSHIP 9-11 © MOLLY POTTER 2008

EXPLORING ATTITUDES, OPINIONS AND VALUES

SEVEN GIFTS (PAGE 32)
Purpose of activity: To explore our values and what could contribute to making a person happy.

Activity notes
Pupils could start by making their choice individually and then try to come to some consensus in pairs, and then in fours to prompt more discussion.

Key discussion points
★ Pupils will choose both things they have and value about themselves and things they would aspire to have.

★ Fun things, like a magic carpet or to be able to make yourself invisible are perfectly valid, as fun is an important part of enjoying life!

★ Most pupils will choose the things they believe would make a person really happy – without realising it. Hopefully discussions will develop towards how each thing would make and keep a person happy.

Extension activities
★ Pupils could consider what they would choose to be the best at in the world and what their wish would be (with a wish for more wishes being banned).

★ Pupils could try and narrow their seven choices down to three.

WHAT ARE WE MEANT TO DO? (PAGE 33)
Purpose of activity: To consider sexual stereotyping and the 'unwritten rules' for males and females.

Key discussion points
★ Society has unwritten rules for several groups of people e.g. the elderly, children, people with disabilities, parents/carers, professionals…etc.

★ Conforming to the unwritten rules and fitting in with stereotypes can make life easier because it is what everyone expects. However, if a person breaks the rules, they can lay themselves open to teasing and criticisms (unfortunately).

★ Although there is pressure on both sexes, there is probably more pressure on males to conform. This can be illustrated using the following example. A girl that likes traditional male pursuits is a tomboy but a boy that is effeminate is likely to be teased.

★ During the teenage years, young people can feel the pressure to conform more intensively than at any other time in their life.

Extension activities
★ Pupils could consider the unwritten rules for other groups of society e.g. old people. It is most easily done by considering what you would never expect an elderly person to do.

★ Pupils could consider further sexual stereotyping by looking at toys, sports, pastimes, different jobs and whether they are considered traditionally male or female. They can then discuss the problems of sexual stereotyping.

★ Pupils could consider how to deal with teasing or insults that result from sexual stereotyping. e.g. a boy being teased for liking dancing, a girl being criticised for being messy and disorganised, a teenage boy being teased for liking school work, a girl that is told she is naughty for losing her temper (even though a boy did it a few minutes earlier and was not told off).

IF YOU COULD… (PAGE 34)
Purpose of the activity: To prompt debate about behaviours that would most benefit a school environment.

Key discussion points
★ Some of the things are about improving relationships and others are about a person feeling better about life. People who feel good about life usually also have better relationships with other people.

Extension activities
★ Pupils could choose one thing from their three – the one they consider to be most important.

★ Pupils might like to think about what they consider to be 'wrong' with the world (e.g. wars, climate change, inequality, lack of empathy, care for others, prejudice) and what personality traits would most impact on these.

★ Pupils could take each one of the qualities or ways of behaving and imagine what a class full of pupils with each one would be like and what the gains (and possible losses) would be.

★ Pupils could design an advert that sells what would be great about their choice.

WHAT'S YOUR OPINION? (PAGE 35)

Purpose of activity: To explore opinions and how they develop.

Key discussion points

★ When people discuss an issue, they can often change their opinion as they think about the topic further, listen to other people's opinions and consider facts they might not have thought or known about before.

★ Most people have strong opinions about one thing or another. The diversity of opinions is something to be celebrated as long as the opinions don't have a negative impact on the rights of others e.g. racist or homophobic opinions.

★ The best way to consider your own opinion about any issue is to try and find out as many facts as you can about it, think about it carefully (possibly discuss it) and then form an opinion.

★ It is OK to be indifferent or undecided about an issue!

Extension activities

★ Pupils could ask several people to complete their questionnaire and display their findings in an interesting way – using different types of graphs, lists, quotes and a commentary on what they think about what they have discovered.

★ Pupils can consider any issue they have strong opinions about themselves. (e.g animal testing, vegetarianism, climate change, school uniform). They can explain why they believe what they do.

★ To show how our opinions can change as we learn more facts about an issue, pupils could be given a topic that they are likely to know little about to explore and form an opinion about e.g. GM foods, nuclear power, censorship, Britain's involvement in Europe, ID cards, left and right wing politics, how best to help homeless people, organ donation, congestion charges.

IS IT WRONG? (PAGE 36)

Purpose of the activity: To consider what makes something 'wrong'.

Key discussion points

★ It is generally believed that if someone deliberately causes harm to another person or denies them their rights, it is wrong.

★ We learn at an early age that something is wrong from the adults in our lives. As we grow up we develop understanding about why something is wrong. As we learn to empathise with others, we can see that things we do can hurt other people.

★ For many of these wrongdoings, you would need to know more information before it could be decided if something was definitely wrong. Some example questions to help consider this are:

   1. Are white lies always wrong?
   2. If someone kills someone in a road accident is it always wrong?
   3. If you try to persuade someone to come to the park and play when they don't want to – is that wrong?
   4. We can all be prejudiced – positively as well as negatively. As long as we actually treat people fairly, is all prejudice automatically wrong?
   5. Teasing can be friendly and if no one is getting upset, is that wrong?

★ Sometimes, in society, whether or not something is wrong or not is not a simple decision. Law courts are used to try and make such decisions.

★ People can decide for themselves whether something is wrong or right for themselves to do. It is best if everyone 'owns' their own moral code. When people try to make decisions for someone else about an issues (e.g. eating meat is wrong), it gets more complicated.

★ People sometimes judge other people's personal moral codes (e.g. some people consider it wrong to live with a person before you are married). If a personal decision does no harm to anyone else, should it definitely be considered as wrong?

Extension activities

★ Pupils could consider how effective punishments are and what works best to help people behave well.

★ You (the teacher) could go into role as a person who is on trial for telling a lie, gossiping, teasing someone or being jealous. You could start by declaring the 'crime' and then let pupils extract more details from you by asking questions. Always plead 'not guilty'. Pupils can eventually pass judgement on whether they believe the deed was wrong or not.

DESERT ISLAND LUXURY (PAGE 37)

Purpose of the activity: To consider the luxuries we often take for granted and to consider those which we most rely upon.

Key discussion points

★ Most people have something they feel they would not be able to live without!

★ Some people might prioritise food, others cleanliness, other the ability to vary things (and not get bored), others entertainment, others comfort and some will have a mixture.

Extension activities

★ Pupils can share their choices and their thinking behind each of the things they chose. They can look at the most popular choices and draw a graph to illustrate what they discovered. Different classes could compare graphs to see how much the discussions in each classroom swayed choices.

WHAT'S YOUR OPINION OF SCHOOL?

WHAT IS AN OPINION?

An opinion is something you believe or a judgement you have made about something that you cannot prove. People can have different opinions on the same topic.

1. Here are some opinions. Do you agree or disagree with them? Discuss with a partner.

'Assemblies are an important part of the school day.'

'I think school would be better if there were no lessons!'

'I think being a teacher must be really hard.'

2. Discuss your opinions about the following topics. See if your opinion changes because of the discussion. If your opinion does change, try and remember what it was that made you change your mind.
   * Do you think punishments are the best way of stopping someone from being naughty?
   * What makes a good school?
   * Is school just about doing work?

3. Devise a questionnaire that investigates pupils' opinions about school. This list might help you think of some questions.
   * Favourite subjects
   * Most important thing to learn
   * What makes a classroom a good place to learn?
   * What is the most important rule?
   * What do pupils admire about teachers?
   * School uniform
   * The best bit of the school day
   * What makes a lesson fun?
   * The best assemblies – and what makes them so good
   * Break times
   * Unhappiness in school
   * Wet break times
   * Naughty children
   * Special occasions – like a school fete, sports day, the school disco

IF THERE IS TIME...

Ask someone to do your questionnaire and see if their answers make you think differently about anything.

PSHE AND CITIZENSHIP 9-11 © MOLLY POTTER 2008

IS IT WRONG?

Taking a person's life	Laughing when someone hurts themselves	Stealing
Gossiping	Deciding things about a person before you know them (prejudice)	Telling a lie
Criticising others	Being rude to your mother, father or carer	Swearing
Bullying	Judging others	Jumping a queue
Trying to persuade someone to do something they don't want to do	Being jealous	Copying homework
Teasing someone	Being two-faced	Hitting someone

Cut out these 'wrongdoings,' and sort them into one of these three groups depending on what you believe about each type of behaviour.
1. ALWAYS WRONG
2. IT DEPENDS
3. NEVER WRONG

NOW DISCUSS THESE QUESTIONS

1. Which of the behaviours would definitely upset or harm another person?
2. Look at any of the behaviours that you have put in 'always wrong' and 'never wrong' – are there any situations in which any of these might move to the 'depends' group?
3. How many of these things have you actually done?
4. From which people or other places, e.g. books or television, can you remember learning that something was 'wrong'?
5. Where have you placed 'judging others'? Have you judged others in this activity?
6. Are there ever times when a person could do one of these things without having chosen to do so?
7. Do you think that different people have different ideas about what is right and wrong and if so – is this O.K?

IF THERE IS TIME...

'You can decide what you think is right and wrong for yourself but you cannot decide for someone else.' Do you agree with this? Discuss your ideas with a partner.

PSHE AND CITIZENSHIP 9–11 © MOLLY POTTER 2008

DESERT ISLAND LUXURY

You are going to be sent to the desert island of Gawaii. It is a beautiful place with sandy beaches, palm trees and a freshwater river. The surrounding sea is crystal clear. The days are always sunny and it only ever rains at night.

On the island there is a cabin for you to live in. Inside the cabin, there is a wooden bed, a wooden chair, a bowl for washing, a toothbrush and paste, a bucket, a cup, a plate, a cooking pot, a knife and a spoon. You have a selection of hats, underwear, trousers, tops and footwear to choose from. You also have some basic tools: a saw, a spade, a lighter, some rope, a sharp knife, some string, a hammer and nails.

On Gawaii, there are plenty of fruit trees and vegetables that grow in the ground. You could survive just by eating these fruit and vegetables and drinking the water from the river.

Before you go to live on Gawaii, you are asked to choose some things from each of the following lists. What do you choose?

SET UP BEFORE YOU ARRIVE

(Choose 3)
* ★ A water system which means that you have a tap in your cabin
* ★ Another room added to the cabin
* ★ A boiler so that you can have hot water
* ★ A light switch that switches a light on in the cabin and one just outside the cabin
* ★ A gas ring on which you can heat food and boil water
* ★ A washing machine for clothes
* ★ A shower

LUXURY ITEMS TO TAKE WITH YOU

(Choose 4)
* ★ A mattress
* ★ A pillow
* ★ An armchair
* ★ A rug for the floor
* ★ A tub big enough for you to sit in
* ★ A large table
* ★ A telescope
* ★ A duvet
* ★ A boat
* ★ A hammock
* ★ Pen and paper
* ★ A towel
* ★ A musical instrument
* ★ A clockwork radio
* ★ An umbrella

REGULAR DELIVERIES

(Choose 5)
These will be delivered once a week.
* ★ Meat
* ★ Chocolate
* ★ Salt
* ★ Rice
* ★ Milk
* ★ Tea and coffee
* ★ Bread
* ★ Pasta
* ★ Soap
* ★ Sugar
* ★ Different herbs and spices
* ★ Butter
* ★ Cheese
* ★ Tissue
* ★ Candles

Draw a picture of each of your choices and write a sentence or two explaining your reason for choosing each thing.

PSHE AND CITIZENSHIP 9–11 © MOLLY POTTER 2008

THE PERFECT PERSON

IMAGINE A PERFECT PERSON

Consider each of the following questions and answer in as much detail as you can.

1. What clothes would the perfect person wear?

2. What colour eyes would a perfect person have?

3. What job would a perfect person do?

4. Would a perfect person be loud or quiet?

5. What kind of things would a perfect person like to learn about?

6. Which emotions would the perfect person feel?

7. Would the perfect person prefer to go to the beach, walk in the countryside or paint a picture?

8. What would the perfect person's friends be like?

9. What kind of things would you never catch the perfect person doing?

10. How would the perfect person describe themselves?

IF THERE IS TIME...

Discuss with a partner: Does a perfect person exist?

PSHE AND CITIZENSHIP 9-11 © MOLLY POTTER 2008

THE QUALITIES SHOP

You are in charge of the Qualities Shop. People come to your shop to buy qualities that make them a better person. You have been given the following price tags and therefore these are the only prices you can use. You need to decide how many Kroop (K) each quality costs.

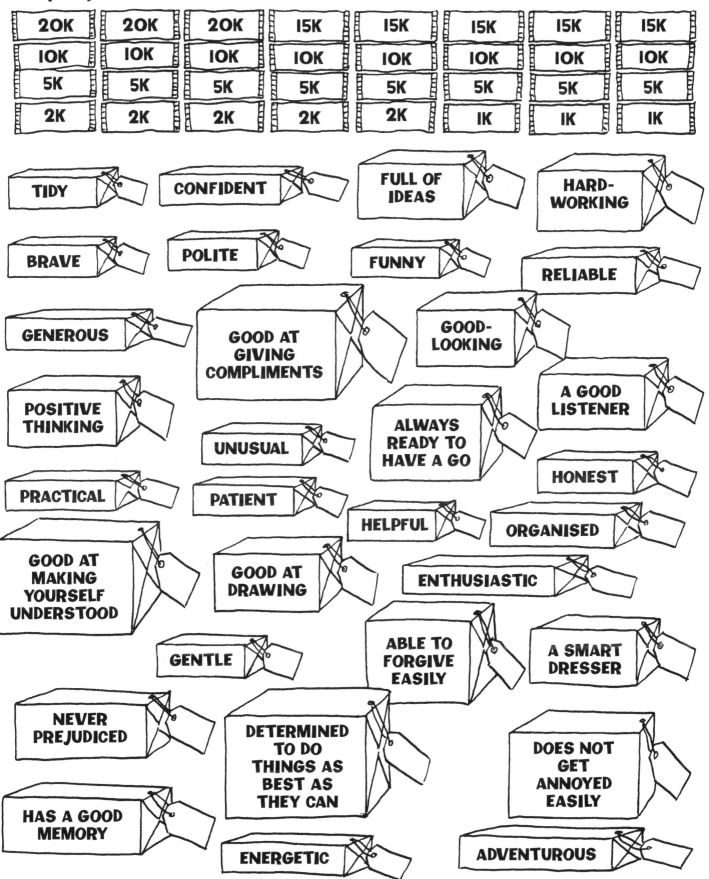

CAN YOU GUESS?

Write the letter of the person you think it is next to each question.

1. Which person is a dentist? ☐

2. Which person is a headteacher? ☐

3. Which person is a teacher? ☐

4. Which person is a car mechanic? ☐

5. Which person has parachuted out of a plane? ☐

6. Which two people are doctors? ☐ and ☐

7. Which two went to university to study music? ☐ and ☐

8. Which person has kept a variety of unusual pets including an eagle, pigs and a squirrel? ☐

9. Which person lives in a caravan in a wood? ☐

10. Which person stays at home and looks after two children? ☐

11. Which person was in the Royal Navy? ☐

12. Which person is vegetarian? ☐

13. Which person is a Catholic? ☐

14. Which person was a clown in the circus? ☐

15. Which person lived in South America for a few years and has travelled a lot? ☐

16. Which person loves fast cars? ☐

PSHE AND CITIZENSHIP 9-11 © MOLLY POTTER 2008

HEALTH AND SAFETY ISSUES

TAKING RISKS (PAGE 44)

Aim of this activity: To consider appropriate risk taking.

Key discussion points

★ Many people stick to what they know to feel safe and secure.

★ Every time we do or learn something new we take the risk of failing or not succeeding immediately. This risk, therefore, has to be taken if we are going to learn new things and have new experiences.

★ Putting our safety unnecessarily at risk is always unwise.

★ Many slightly risky things can be made safer by the actions we take e.g. putting a seatbelt on in a car or wearing a bicycle helmet. If you can reduce risk from harm, then it is wise to do so.

★ Some decisions in life mean that we take long-term risk – like buying a house.

★ Sometimes when we do something, all we are risking is being criticised or laughed at – but if we don't feel good about ourselves, this can feel like a huge risk to take. It takes confidence to take risks.

★ There is little or no adventure unless you take risks!

Extension activities

★ Pupils could draw a risk map of their route to school and label how they keep risk to a minimum e.g. using pedestrian crossings, not crossing near a corner or parked cars.

★ Pupils could consider good and bad risk i.e. good means you try new things, bad is when you put your safety needlessly at risk.

★ Pupils could make, 'take a risk' posters that encourage people to have a go at trying new things and challenging themselves out of their comfort zone.

SAFETY SUSAN (PAGE 45)

Purpose of the activity:

To consider danger and how to minimise risk.

Key discussion points

★ We can never live our lives in a 100% safety (or we would never move!) but there are things we can do to minimise risk.

★ Pupils could fill in a table like this. Some examples have been included for you.

Extension activities

★ Pupils could write Safety Susan's guide to cycling.

★ Pupils could look at safety signs and consider the hazards they warn us about.

★ Pupils can consider the rules and procedures that keep them safe in school.

★ Pupils could separate the hazards on the sheet into two groups: indoors and outdoors. They could then write a guide to keeping safe – for indoors or outdoors.

TO DO OR NOT TO DO? (PAGE 46)

Purpose of activity: To raise awareness of other people's influence on the things you decide to do.

Key discussion points

★ Many people are influenced by other people to make 'bad' decisions. Peer pressure and peer influence can be very powerful.

★ To stick to what you truly want to do and be true to yourself takes confidence and sometimes, bravery.

★ The need to 'fit in' is particularly strong in the teenage years.

★ People usually admire a person who is not easily influenced by other people.

Extension activities

★ Pupils could choose one of the scenarios (B or D) and discuss how a person could get out of doing what they are being pressurised to do.

★ Pupils could also consider how they could behave more responsibly in scenario A.

★ Pupils could write advice about dealing with peer pressure and influence e.g. do something because you want to, resist pressure from others, have the guts to be different, be respected for being someone who is true to yourself.etc.

Potential hazards	What is the danger	What can be done to minimise risk?
Railway	Death or injury	Never trespass on or near railways
Candle	Burning from hot wax, setting room alight	Make sure you put the candle in a holder that keeps the candle securely upright. Never tip the candle over.
Boiling kettle Boiling pan	Scalding from the steam or boiling water	Do not go near steam. Pour kettle or pan with extreme care
Cooking hob	burning	Never touch a cooking hob unless you are certain it is cool
Building site	Falling materials, slipping, getting cut, breaking limbs	Never play on building sites
Toaster	Burning, getting an electric shock	Never touch the element. Always wait for the toast to pop up before getting it out.
Bleach	Burning, poisoning	Never play with household cleaning materials

AGE LIMITS (PAGE 47)

Purpose of activity: To consider the laws that are in place to protect children and young people and how effective they are.

Answers:

The age at which you are legally allowed to:

work part time	14 – there are also restrictions on the hours that can be worked at this age.
buy a lottery ticket	16
get married with parents'/carers' permission	16 and 18 without parents'/carers' permission
buy alcohol	18
adopt a child	21
buy fireworks	18 – there are some 'children's fireworks, that can be bought at a younger age
leave home without your parents'/carers' permission	16
go in a bar and drink soft drinks	14
buy cigarettes	18
learn to drive a car	17

Key discussion points

★ The laws aim to protect children and young people from a variety of hazards (e.g. health hazards – the younger you start smoking the more likely you will develop smoking related illnesses, firework burns, getting addicted to gambling, car accidents through lack of competency with driving…etc)

★ The laws alone do not protect people from these hazards – especially as adults can legally be at risk from each hazard. Education about each issue is also very important if people are to minimise risks.

★ Some young people get a thrill from doing something that is illegal for their age group. Some people might argue that these laws make things seem more attractive and exciting to some young people.

★ Some laws could not possibly be policed thoroughly and their upkeep is dependent on social pressure and stigmas. e.g. drink driving, speeding.

★ Some examples of laws that aim to protect adults are: smoking no longer allowed in enclosed spaces, being illegal to drive when drunk, being illegal not to wear a seat belt…etc

Extension activities

★ Pupils could look at the age limits of other countries for each of the laws in the table.

★ Pupils could debate the question, 'do laws work?'

HEALTHY HETTY (PAGE 48)

Purpose of activity: To consider what a healthy lifestyle would be like and what changes could be made to your own lifestyle to make it healthier.

Key discussion points

★ A healthy adult lifestyle would have a balanced diet with plenty of fruit and veg, a diet with about 70 grammes for women and 90 grammes for men of fat a day, a little salt and no or very little sugar, regular exercise (1/2 hour a day), no smoking (direct or passive), no or little alcohol intake, regular sleep (about 8 hours each 24), about 8 glasses of water (or fluids) a day and little or no stress, some time made for relaxation and attention paid to maintaining happiness (e.g. talking worries through with friends).

★ We often develop habits for life at a young age.

★ The effects of unhealthy lifestyles can be seen in children in the form of poor concentration, being unfit, obesity, poor dental health etc.

★ The long term risks to health include heart attacks, diabetes, gum disease, cancer, poor mental health, strokes etc but these are unlikely to happen before middle adulthood.

★ A child's healthy lifestyle would be similar to the adult's above but with more sleep and no alcohol.

Extension Activities

★ Pupils can investigate what things can actually prevent people from making healthy choices in their lives by using a questionnaire or consider what a character called Unhealthy Una would do and say about each of the issues on the sheet e.g. fatty food is more tasty, habits are hard to change, poor health choices can be imposed on you, exercise is boring etc.

★ Pupils could design a campaign involving Healthy Hetty.

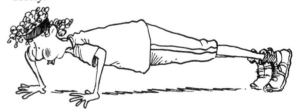

TO SMOKE OR NOT TO SMOKE? (PAGE 49)

Purpose of the activity: To consider the reasons why some people start smoking.

Key discussion points

★ There is a tendency in education and health to try and shock young people into not smoking. This assumes people only start smoking because they don't know it is harmful.

★ It is hard for children and young people to see the long-term health impacts of smoking and it is unlikely to be in the forefront of their minds if they ever have to make the decision to smoke or not.

★ If we perceive our peers are all doing something, even if they're not, this can make us want to do it too! Sometimes health promotion messages can make smoking seem like more of a problem than it is and give the impression that more people smoke than actually do.

★ Being directly pressurised into smoking is not that common.

★ If someone decides they are not going to be a smoker, they might need to be prepared to be determined about it – especially if at times it seems like everyone is smoking.

Extension activities

★ Pupils could act out their adverts.

★ Pupils could make a magazine advert to complement the TV one.

★ Pupils could design a questionnaire that explores attitudes towards smoking.

STRESS (PAGE 50)

Purpose of activity: To understand what stress is, the effect it can have and how to deal with it.

Key discussion points

★ Nearly everyone suffers from stress several times in their life. Sustained stress over a long period of time can be damaging to a person's health.

★ Many different things can cause stress. Pupils may have heard adults talking about feeling stressed and be aware of what has caused that stress. Going for a walk, lying on a beach and being given a present, however, are rarely causes of stress!

★ Different people show stress in different ways and there are lots of different stress symptoms.

★ Different people find different ways of dealing with stress. A person can either deal with the cause (if possible) or find ways of relaxing and 'switching off' the stress. Examples of switching off the stress include: exercise, listening to music, meditation (e.g. focusing on breathing, or on this moment only), reading, painting a picture, stroking a pet, etc.

Extension activities

★ Pupils could write a guide to relaxation.

★ Pupils could research information about stress on the internet – finding out other symptoms and causes of stress and ways to deal with it.

WHAT MAKES US HAPPY? (PAGE 51)

Purpose of the activity: To explore the idea of what does or does not contribute to a person's happiness.

Activity notes

This activity is easier to do if pupils cut each card out.

Key discussion points

★ Many people consider material wealth (beyond a person's basic needs being met) as having little impact on a person's happiness.

★ The kind of things that seem to contribute towards a person's happiness are: a positive outlook, self-esteem and resilience, support networks, etc.

★ No one can expect to be completely happy all of the time. Things happen to make us experience negative emotions - we would only worry if a person remained extremely unhappy for a long period of time. This activity just refers to a tendency towards contentedness in life.

Extension activities

★ Pupils could make a child-friendly school 'Happiness Policy'.

★ Pupils could consider what activities might be included in a school 'gigglethon.'

HOW ARE YOU FEELING? (PAGE 52)

Purpose of the activity: To help to develop the skill of describing how they feel and to consider the benefits of this.

Key discussion points

★ In most situations, finding someone who will listen to how you feel can help.

★ Suffering in silence or bottling up your feelings is never a good thing to do.

★ Traditionally, sharing your feelings is seen as a very female thing to do and social conditioning can make boys reluctant to do so – unless it's anger. This can cause a lot of suffering and both sexes need to be encouraged to share their feelings.

★ Emotional literacy and empathy are parts of intra and inter-personal intelligence.

★ Emotions are emotions and cannot be helped. We do, however, have control over how we react to emotions. e.g. if someone makes us angry, we could either hit them or we could choose to calm ourselves down and then tell them assertively that what they did made us angry.

★ Sometimes the people we share how we are feeling with do not listen attentively and therefore do not necessarily make us feel any better. If this is the case, it is a good idea to find someone else to talk to, and if they don't help, find someone else and so on.

Extension activities

★ Pupils can investigate what 'the ideal person to share your worries with' would be like. What qualities would this person have and how would they listen to you?

★ Pupils could choose an emotion (from the bottom of the pupils' page) and draw a cartoon scenario that shows a person feeling that way. This could be made into a 'Feelings Book'.

★ Pupils could play guess the emotion by either doing individual freeze-frames where they focus on facial expression and body language, they could describe the emotion or they could draw a picture that represents it.

★ Pupils can paint abstract representations of different emotions and use similes and metaphors to describe them. Pupils could also speculate what an emotion might sound, taste, feel, look and smell like.

★ Pupils could reflect upon yesterday and try to remember the many different emotions they had and what caused them.

TAKING RISKS

Everyone has to take risks in their lives. If we didn't, we would end up doing very little. However, there are different types of risks. Here are five different types of risk:

Very, very little or no risk e.g. doing everything the same as you always have done. **A**	Slight risk but no real danger to your safety e.g. learning something new. **B**	Risk for a thrill but you feel in control e.g. going on a fairground ride. **C**	A big risk to get something you think you want in the long run e.g. buying a house. **D**	A risk to your safety that you feel out of control of e.g. getting in the car of a person who has been drinking alcohol. **E**

1. Consider the risks below with a partner and decide...
★ Which type of risk (from **A** to **E** above) you think each one is.
★ What the risk or danger actually is – if there is one?

Climbing a tall tree

Going go-cart racing

A grown up moving to another country to live.

Trying a new food that looks really slimy!

Getting into the car of someone you don't know

A grown up leaving their job in the hope of getting a new one

Choosing a friend you know you get on with when your teacher asks you to find a partner

Leaving the football club that you have really enjoyed so you can go to Karate because it is on the same night

Offering to read something out in assembly even though you have never done it before and you know you will be nervous

2. Depending on what you believe, answer true or false to the following statements.

	True	False
A 'risk' is a risk because you cannot be sure what will happen.		
It would be a good idea to never take any risk in your life.		
Every time you try something new, you are taking a risk.		
It is sensible not to take a risk that could mean you might be very unsafe.		
You can always tell straight away whether or not the risk you took was a good or bad idea.		
Before you take a risk, it is a good idea to think about it for a while — if there is time.		
Sometimes people don't take risks because they are scared of what people will think or say.		
Every risk you take will turn out well.		

IF THERE IS TIME...

No-Risk-Roger never, ever takes risks. He sticks to what he knows and never tries out anything new. He does pretty much the same thing every day. If anyone suggests he has a go at something, he always refuses.
With a partner, make a list of all the things you both would not have done in your life if you been No-Risk-Roger! See how many you can think of.

PSHE AND CITIZENSHIP 9-11 © MOLLY POTTER 2008

Safety Susan is the most safety aware person you are ever likely to meet. Because she is so concerned about safety, she has made a theme park with lots of possible dangers and she gives children guided tours. She points out all the hazards, talks about how to avoid them and how to keep safe.

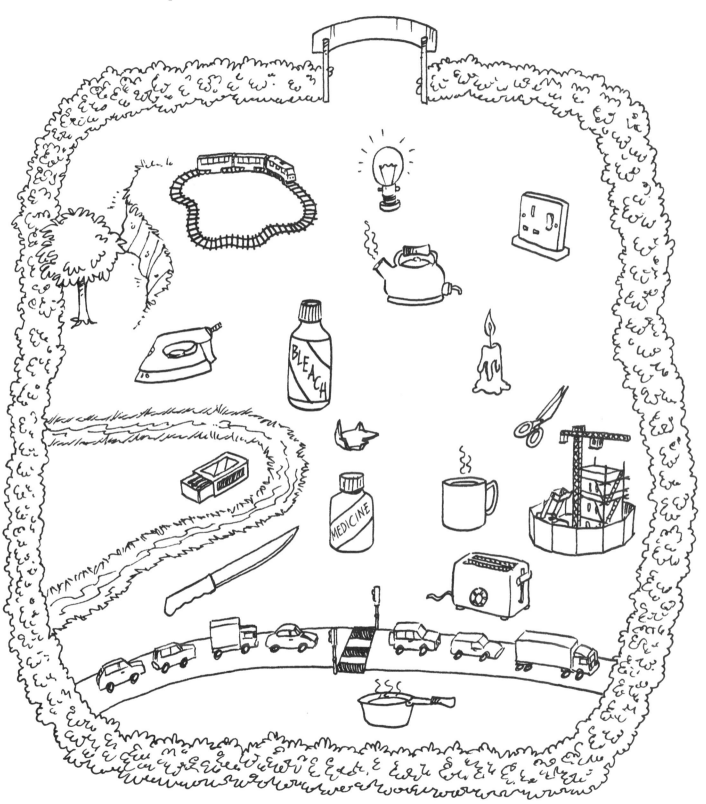

PSHE AND CITIZENSHIP 9-11 © MOLLY POTTER 2008

For each hazard work out what Susan would say about:
1. What the danger is.
2. What a person needs to do to keep safe.

TO DO OR NOT TO DO?

Many people have done things for negative reasons.

Put the following decisions into this table. You might put some decisions in more than one row.
a) Laughing at someone who is being teased by a crowd of people.
b) Accepting a cigarette that someone is persuading you to smoke.
c) Spending a fortune on fashionable clothing.
d) Doing something you have been dared to do, even though it's dangerous.
e) Teasing someone in front of a crowd.
f) Staying in the park with your friends and going home later than you were told to.

REASON A PERSON MIGHT DO SOMETHING	AN EXAMPLE OF THE KIND OF THING A PERSON MIGHT DO BECAUSE OF THIS REASON
Someone had pressurised them into doing it.	
Everyone around them is doing it.	
They are worried about what other people will think of them if they don't.	
They think it will make them look cool.	
They are scared to be different.	

TALK ABOUT...

1. What advice would you give to someone who did things just because they were worried about what other people thought of them?
2. Make a list of positive reasons for deciding to do something e.g.
   ★ because a person wants to get good at something
   ★ because a person really enjoys something

Work with a partner. Which of the following do you think are necessary for someone to be happy? Can you number them from most necessary (1) to least (20)?

Owning lots of things	Not taking unimportant things too seriously
Not thinking too much about things that have already happened and moving on	Lots of money
Learning from mistakes	Not to worry too much about things
Friends that you can have fun with	Friends that are supportive when you are sad
People that love you whatever you do	Being a kind person
Enough food and drink	Having holidays
Not being easily irritated	Having a home
Living in a big house	Being really good at something
Being good at spending time on your own	Knowing what you like doing
Being grateful for what you have – 'counting your blessings'	Being an optimist

1. Which things caused lots of discussion?
2. Design a 'Be Happy' poster with at least six pieces of advice to people on how to be happy.

IF THERE IS TIME...

Present your 'Be Happy' poster to the class and talk about the advice you have put on it.

PSHE AND CITIZENSHIP 9-11 © MOLLY POTTER 2008

HOW ARE YOU FEELING?

It's a great skill to be able to describe how you are feeling and an even better one to be able explain it to other people. Telling other people, particularly about negative feelings, can often make people feel better.

Work with a partner and describe in as much detail as you can, how you think you would feel in each of the following situations. Sometimes you might feel a mixture of emotions.

You are told off for something you didn't do and when you try to explain that you didn't do it, no one believes you.

When you arrive at school, you discover that the lunch time club that you love going to has been cancelled.

Your mum/dad/carer tells you thatthere will be a surprise waiting for you when you get home.

You go to meet a friend that you have arranged to meet at the park but they don't turn up.

It is your birthday tomorrow and you are not sure if you have been bought the only present you really wanted to get.

You are called up in assembly because you have received a very special award. You know your friend was hoping to receive that very award.

You are trying to do a maths sum but you really cannot get it. Everyone around you seems to get it really easily.

When you cross the road a car drives past you really fast and toots its horn at you.

You discover that a close friend has been moaning about you behind your back.

You have a difficult maths test later that day. Your friend tells you that he is really looking forward to it.

You forget your line in the school play in front of the whole school even though you only had one.

Someone in your class teases you about the shoes you are wearing.

You join a new club with 30 members and you do not know a single person there.

You forgot your PE kit but the school secretary tells you that someone has dropped it off at the school.

Some feeling words to help you:

Happy	Excited	Surprised	Concerned	Unsure
Hopeful	Sad	Unsettled	Awkward	Satisfied
Confused	Embarrassed	Proud	Disgusted	Tense
Angry	Grateful	Indifferent	Furious	Insecure
Frightened	Disappointed	Regretful	Nervous	Relieved
Worried	Annoyed	Tempted	Bored	Guilty
Frustrated	Jealous	Alarmed	Panicked	Agitated

THE WORLD AROUND US

INSPECTION! (PAGE 56)
Purpose of activity: To help pupils reflect upon what happens at playtime and consider and suggest any possible improvements.

Activity notes
Pupils can comment on the areas outlined in the table and use the questions to guide their comments. Encourage pupils to also make general comments about what they observe. You might like to split your class into five groups and have a different batch of inspectors – one for each day of the week and take feedback and summarise findings at the end of the week.

Key discussion points
★ Pupils might stumble upon a problem - the resolution of which can be discussed and possibly implemented – if appropriate.

Extension activities
★ If pupils all agree that playtime is generally excellent, they could write a newspaper report – outlining the findings that support this.

★ Pupils could design an inspection form and inspect one of the following: wet break, assembly, a lesson.

★ Pupils could plan an assembly to report what they found out about break times to the whole school.

HOW THE STORY IS TOLD (PAGE 57)
Purpose of the activity: To highlight to pupils how the media can and does portray the same story from different viewpoints.

Key discussion points
★ One story focuses on the aggressive trespasser and the other focuses on the fact that a right of way has been denied.

★ To make them less angry: Mr Hibbly could be told about the right of way and Mr Trevor could be told that Mr Hibbly had only just moved in and therefore was not responsible for the obstructions to the right of way.

★ The editor of a newspaper can influence what his or her reader will believe about a story or an issue.

★ Some papers always report certain issues with a bias.

★ Newspaper reporters have to write quickly and will not have time to find out all the facts about a story. They are happy if they have a story that is interesting to read.

★ We need to consider anything we read in the paper carefully and not automatically assume that what we are reading is the whole story.

Extension activities
Pupils could look at real newspaper stories and
★ look for differences in how the stories are reported
★ make up some questions that they would like answered to be sure they have a fair report of a story
★ alter a story so that a different viewpoint is given

★ look at a story whilst donning a 'different hat' – an old person, a teenager, a teacher, a parent/carer etc.

★ look for groups of people that some papers regularly pick on such as Travellers, teenagers or single mothers.

ADVERT INVESTIGATION (PAGE 58)
Purpose of activity: To explore the messages adverts give us and how they can sometimes make us feel bad about ourselves.

Activity notes
This activity can be extended significantly if pupils are given a selection of magazine adverts. They can choose one of the four 'personas' listed and produce a collage/poster of messages and images they can find that would annoy their chosen persona.

Key discussion points
★ Adverts can put pressure on people to conform to a very narrow idea of what is attractive, acceptable and appealing to others.

★ Adverts' sole aim is to get you to buy their product and they employ a variety of techniques to persuade people to do this. e.g. the product is luxurious, if you buy the product you will be more attractive, the product will make you more successful or better than others etc.

Extension activities
★ Pupils could draw the advert their 'persona' would draw to promote their message.

★ Pupils could develop a set of questions that would help someone to look at adverts and the messages they give, in a discerning way e.g. does the advert only use attractive people? Is the advert making you feel like you are a bad parent if you do not buy the product? etc.

ADVERT PEOPLE! (PAGE 59)
Purpose of the activity: To consider what models in adverts could leave us believing is 'normal' and to challenge this.

Activity notes
It is useful if pupils can look at a few adverts from glossy magazines that contain people.

Key discussion points
★ 'Advert men' and 'women' rarely look very 'real' and very few real people look like they are from an advert!

★ The purpose of adverts is to sell something. To catch people's eye, they use artificially perfect looking people.

★ Many 'advert people' have been digitally enhanced with computer software.

★ If a person compared themselves to 'advert people' they would be sure to feel less than perfect. Most people feel positive about some aspects about their bodies – it is better to focus on these aspects. We all need to learn to accept ourselves as we are – it can make a person very unhappy if they don't learn to do this.

★ It is a wonderful thing that we all look different – it makes the world a more interesting place - and we need to celebrate this!

★ People find different things attractive. Attractiveness is not based solely on what people look like – personality plays a big part in how attractive a person is. A smile can make someone more attractive.

★ Even if you do not feel completely happy with the way you look, it is a good idea not to be afraid to express your 'style' by wearing clothes that you think reflect who you are rather than trying to be something you are not!

Extension activities

★ Pupils could take a picture of an 'advert person' and make him/her more 'real' by drawing on to it. They could include thought bubbles showing the person worrying about going home in heavy traffic, creases in their clothes, some messy hair etc.

★ Ask pupils to stand on an 'agreement spectrum' line depending on how they feel about the following statements. After each pupil has stood on the 'agreement spectrum', ask, 'does anyone want to say anything about where they have stood?' to develop discussion.

    a. I think that most people do not look like the people in adverts.

    b. I think that adverts can make people feel bad about their bodies.

    c. I think most people are happy with the way they look.

    d. I think it is difficult to feel positive about the way you look.

    e. I think people should try and feel positive about their bodies whatever shape and size they are.

CAN YOU BELIEVE IT? (PAGE 60)

Purpose of activity: To consider what adverts aim to do, how they do it and to challenge their messages.

Key discussion points

★ Adverts' sole purpose is to persuade the consumer to buy their product.

★ As products are in competition with each other, a lot of money is spent on deciding how to promote each product to try and make it sound great and better than all others.

★ Although, legally, adverts are not allowed to lie or claim their product does something it does not actually do, there are still ways of 'exaggerating' the effectiveness of a product.

★ Adverts use lots of different techniques to sell their product and/or to get you to look at them such as:

    1. An eye catching picture.

    2. Making you seem clever or sophisticated if you buy it.

    3. Baffling you with science that makes the product sound very effective.

    4. A catchy slogan used in every advert: billboard, magazine, T.V.

    5. Trying to make you feel guilty if you chose not to have the product – which is made to look like an absolute necessity e.g. household hygiene products aimed at parents.

    6. Making you think you have a real bargain.

    7. Making the product look amazing and seem like a really great idea.

    8. Puzzling you to make you intrigued.

    9. Asking a question to get you interested.

★ Occasionally a product is produced that is unique and different from anything else – advertising works very successfully to sell these products.

★ It is wise to remember the purpose of adverts and keep a discerning eye when it comes to the messages they deliver!

Extension activities

★ Pupils could look at a selection of adverts and investigate the different techniques that have been used to sell each product.

★ Pupils could cover a real advert in 'graffiti' or draw their own advert from scratch - so that it just makes the product sound ordinary – which is what it probably is!

GET OUT OF THE CAR! (PAGE 61)

Purpose of activity: To consider the most effective way of persuading people to travel less by car for short journeys.

Key discussion points

★ If something is to realistically be done about climate change, it is believed that lifestyle changes will need to be made. Cars are just a part of all that contributes to climate change.

★ In many towns and cities, traffic is very heavy and many people would actually arrive more quickly at their destination if they cycled.

★ Cycling and walking keeps you fit!

★ Taking the bus means you don't have to worry about parking and in some cities, bus lanes can mean the bus arrives at the destination more quickly than a car would.

Extension activities

★ Pupils could discuss what is meant by carbon footprint.

★ Pupils could discuss what changes could happen to public transport to make it more user friendly.

★ Pupils could discuss how cycling could be made a more attractive means of travelling to everyone.

★ A lot of short journey traffic is due to children being dropped off at school. (Some parents/carers then continue driving on to work after the school run.) Pupils could look at ways of reducing this particular short journey in a car – including car sharing.

★ Pupils could design posters and leaflets and a radio advert that delivers their campaign's message.

PERSUADE THEM TO SLOW DOWN! (PAGE 62)

Purpose of the activity: To consider how to influence people to think about what they are doing and to change their habits.

Activity notes

Encourage pupils to discuss lots of ideas before they settle on one. Some ideas they could develop are:

★ A letter as if it was written from a child that is scared of crossing the road.

★ A leaflet quite clearly expressing the increased likelihood of injuring or killing someone if they are hit at higher speeds and how high speeds increase the likelihood of someone getting hit.

★ Something that illustrates stopping distances at different speeds.

★ Something that explains that good driving is careful driving.

★ Something that explains that although you do not usually encounter something dangerous, it only takes one incident.

★ A way of reminding drivers to keep an eye on their speedometer.

Key discussion points:

★ Pupils could start by considering the reasons for people speeding.

1. They are not concentrating on their speed.
2. They think fast driving equates to good or confident driving.
3. They like to go fast.
4. They are not aware of the potential hazards.
5. They believe that all pedestrians will take care when they cross the road.
6. Because everyone does it, it would be pointless if they slowed down.
7. They really don't think of other people.

★ Pupils can also consider what is wrong with speeding

1. Safety – you are more likely hurt or kill someone if you hit them as speed.
2. Stopping distances – the faster you go the longer it takes you to stop and the greater the distance you will travel after you have put the brakes on.
3. If you are speeding, you are less likely to see potential hazards.
4. It makes pedestrians feel unsafe.

Extension activities

★ Pupils could draw a sticker that is linked to their postal campaign that could be stuck on to a steering wheel.

★ Pupils could design a speed limit sign that tries to persuade people to keep to the speed limit.

THE POWER OF THE CONSUMER (PAGE 63)

Purpose of the activity: To consider the buying choices people make and their reasons for doing so.

Key discussion points

★ There are a variety of concerns that could be considered when buying food. Different people have different priorities.

★ Some people say that the power of the consumer is the most direct influence people in rich countries can have.

Extension activities

★ Pupils could rank the issues from most to least significant. They can do this in anticipation of the kind of shopper they think they will be when they grow up.

★ Pupils could make 'the power of the consumer poster' that illustrates all the key issues covered in this activity.

CONFLICT (PAGE 64)

Purpose of activity: To consider conflict and what does and does not help to resolve it.

Key discussion points

★ If conflict is fuelled, it can continue and escalate for a long time.

★ Resolving conflict is about finding a positive way forward that both sides want – rather than dwelling on what caused the conflict in the first place. The best conflict resolutions are not about winning and losing.

★ If the discussion was had again (with the idea of sorting out whether the sky or the sea was best for once and for all) this would fuel the conflict – especially as it is a ridiculous debate.

★ Education can help people to tolerate or even celebrate the fact people have different points of view.

★ It you prevent people from being allowed to believe and talk about what they want this is a big affront to freedom of speech.

★ If a wall were to be built it would be a restriction on people's freedom.

★ If one of the laws were made, resentment would build up and the conflict would continue. Plus, there would be no fair way of deciding whether the law should be in the Jyes or the Jees favour.

Extension activities

★ Pupils could imagine what would happen if a wall were built. How would the Jees start to remember the Jyes and vice versa. Encourage the pupils to exaggerate!

★ Pupils could design a lesson that could be delivered to the children on the island to encourage them to tolerate a different point of view.

★ Pupils could write a charter for the island that, if everyone signed it, would be the end to the conflict.

★ Pupils could role-play a Jye and a Jee talking about the sky and the sea - pre and post conflict.

INSPECTION!

You are a school inspector. You are going to inspect an outdoor playtime. You need to write a report about what you find. You might need to interview some pupils to do this well.

Here is the report file you are going to use to write your report. Observe a playtime in your school and fill in the report in as much detail as possible.

GRADING

Excellent	A
Good	B
Average	C
Poor	D
Awful!	E

	YOUR COMMENTS	overall grading
ACTIVITY Are most children happy with what they are doing at playtime? Is there a choice of things to do? Does one activity take over and if so, is this OK?		
COMING IN FROM BREAK Do pupils come in from break safely? Do the smaller children feel safe? Is there any pushing and shoving?		
THE STAFF ON PLAYGROUND DUTY Do the staff on duty pay attention to what is happening on the playground?		
CHILDREN'S BEHAVIOUR Generally do the pupils behave well at playtime? Are pupils supportive of each other – for example, if a pupil is hurt or upset are they looked after well? Does anyone get left out?		
PLAYTIME RULES What playtime rules are there? Is everyone aware of these rules and the reasons for them? Do pupils generally follow the rules?		
OVERALL Do pupils generally look forward to playtime? What, if anything, would pupils say needs improving about playtime? Anything else?		

PSHE AND CITIZENSHIP 9-11 © MOLLY POTTER 2008

Newspapers have reports so people can learn about what has happened. Newspapers also look for ways to tell a story so that it is as interesting as it can possibly be, so that the paper sells well. This can sometimes mean that one viewpoint is strongly pushed forward. Read these reports about the same incident.

AGGRESSIVE TRESSPASSER SHOUTS AT LANDOWNER

Mr Hibbly was said to be angry and shaken after he encountered a trespasser walking next to the River Flare that winds across his 20 acres of land. He told the Flareford News how he had approached the trespasser and asked what he was doing only to be shouted at and told that he had no right to be asking any questions.

Mr Hibbly, who moved into his current house just two days ago, immediately returned to the house to phone the police. Unfortunately, when the police arrived, the trespasser was nowhere to be seen. All that was left was a sign implying that the trespassing was perfectly OK. Mr Hibbly said, "I find it really strange to think that someone can just march on to my land and shout at me. It really does make you wonder about people nowadays."

Mr Hibbly does not wish to investigate this incident any further.

PUBLIC RIGHT OF WAY HAS BEEN HIDDEN FOR A DECADE

This weekend, Mr James Trevor of Highgate Road attempted to reclaim the public right of way that runs alongside the River Flare.
"I was sure that we used to walk by the river when I was a child and I wondered why people no longer did,' he said.

Mr Trevor spent some time in the local records office investigating the disappearance of the footpath and found that there was, in fact, a public right of way along the river. He used the map, he had found later that day, to trace the route of the footpath but found that many obstacles had been deliberately placed along the path.

"At one point I found a mesh of barbed wire in my way. As I walked along the route I became more and more angry about someone's attempt to obscure the public footpath. These footpaths need to be protected."

1. What is the main focus of each story?

2. What could Mr Trevor and Mr Hibbly be told about this situation to make them both less angry about what happened?

3. Why do you think newspaper reporters don't always bother to get all the facts before they write a report?

4. Discuss and then write two short newspaper reports that give different points of view about one of the following situations.
* ★ The reason why a restaurant manager insisted a man should leave the building.
* ★ A conflict that has broken out between two neighbours over some land.
* ★ The reason why a shopkeeper had to close down his shop even though the local people wanted it to remain open as the nearest supermarket was further to travel to.

IF THERE IS TIME...
Most stories have at least two sides to them. Discuss the advice you might give someone about not always believing everything that is written in a newspaper.

PSHE AND CITIZENSHIP 9-11 © MOLLY POTTER 2008

THE PERFECT GIFT

....luxury for the bathroom.

THIS BEAUTIFULLY PACKAGED GIFT IS THE PERFECT OPPORTUNITY TO SPOIL SOMEONE YOU LOVE. CONTAINS LUXURY SOAP AND BUBBLE BATH. ORDER BY POST. SEND THE FOLLOWING COUPON TO: LUXURY: PO BOX 1, SOAPLAND.

① Coupon

BE YOUNG AGAIN...

MAGIC MOISTURISER - applied daily will takes years off you. Look ten years younger!

GET THE LIFESTYLE...

SHOP AT FORBES FOR A HOUSE THAT SHOWS OFF JUST WHO YOU ARE!

LOOK LIKE A MODEL

Clothes from Mr. Model.

GET THE RIGHT LOOK.

Discuss with a partner which messages in these adverts might annoy the following people:

★ **Someone who believes in recycling, reducing packaging, repairing goods and reducing pollution.**

★ **Someone who celebrates the fact that we are all different.**

★ **Someone who believes happiness is not about owning lots of things.**

★ **Someone who believes that your appearance is nowhere as important as your personality.**

PSHE AND CITIZENSHIP 9-11 © MOLLY POTTER 2008

ADVERT PEOPLE!

MALE | FEMALE

If an alien landed on planet earth and found a pile of glossy magazines, what would they be led to believe humans looked like? Draw a picture and label the features of the average 'advert man' and the average 'advert woman'.

CONSIDER

★ colour of skin
★ attractiveness
★ ability/disability
★ size
★ age
★ hair
★ skin

★ possessions
★ clothes
★ how attractive others find them
★ their emotions
★ lifestyle
★ leisure interests

DISCUSS

★ How does the 'average' person compare with the 'advert' people?
★ How might these 'advert' people make some people feel about themselves and their lives?
★ What could you say to the alien to persuade it that 'real' people are better than the advert people?

PSHE AND CITIZENSHIP 9-11 © MOLLY POTTER 2008

HARPEEN

The best washing up liquid you are ever likely to use! Leaves your dishes sparkling!

Cleans like no other liquid.
Dishes so clean you'll need sunglasses!
HARPEEN CLEANS MEAN

Are your dishes clean enough?
Use **Sparkle**

The washing up liquid that will mean you never want to use another!

Protect your family. Get your dishes healthily clean with **Sparkle**.

NEW IMPROVED

ZAPS SUDS

Our scientists have been working night and day to bring you a washing up liquid that beats all others. The new X546 formula is our secret ingredient. No one else knows about it!

A must for modern living...
Kleen-o-dish

Our new, stylish handy-grip bottle will add style to your kitchen.
This month s offer
Buy one get one free!

1. **What are adverts trying to do?**
2. **In these adverts can you spot...**
   - ★ **A slogan to help you remember the name of the product**
   - ★ **A bargain**
   - ★ **Trying to impress you with science**
   - ★ **Making you feel guilty if you don't buy it**
   - ★ **Something that claims their product has been made even better than it was**
   - ★ **Claims that this product is better than all others**
   - ★ **A hint that you are stylish if you buy it**
3. **Would you believe all of these adverts?**

PSHE AND CITIZENSHIP 9-11 © MOLLY POTTER 2008

GET OUT OF THE CAR!

ABOUT A THIRD OF ALL JOURNEYS MADE IN THE CAR ARE LESS THAN TWO MILES.

Here are some things people said about travelling in the car for short journeys:

"With three young kids, it would take a lot of organisation to get anywhere if I didn't use the car."

"I'd have to leave much earlier if I didn't drive – although sometimes finding somewhere to park takes a long time."

"I don't much like sitting in traffic jams, but I'd rather be in my own car in a traffic jam than on a bus."

Think about the advantages and disadvantages of each of the following ways of travelling a two mile journey and complete this table.

WAY OF TRAVELLING	ADVANTAGES	DISADVANTAGES
WALKING		
CYCLING		
TAKING THE BUS		
GOING IN A CAR		

IF THERE IS TIME...

Discuss what message you would use if you were in charge of a campaign to persuade people to use their cars less. Try to make it a message that would really make people think about using their car less.

PSHE AND CITIZENSHIP 9-11 © MOLLY POTTER 2008

PERSUADE THEM TO SLOW DOWN!

In a small town known as **Rodston** there is a terrible problem, many cars are speeding. The speed limit on all roads with housing is twenty miles an hour but this appears to be ignored by nearly everyone. **Rodston** Town Council has decided to post a letter or a leaflet to every home in the town to try and persuade everyone to stop speeding.

A few people that were caught speeding were asked why they had done so. Their replies were,

"Everyone here does it. Why should I be different?"

"It's easy to forget to pay attention to the speed you are doing."

"I like to drive fast – I've got a sports car— it doesn't bother anyone."

"Only old people drive slowly because they are not very good at driving."

"I'd be able to stop quickly if I needed to."

"Children are taught the green cross code, they know to look for cars before they cross the road."

YOUR TASK

You have been asked to produce the leaflet or letter that will be posted through every letterbox in **Rodston**.

You will need to consider:
   ★ You can only use paper to print your messages on to.
   ★ You need to decide if you are going to use an envelope or not and if you use an envelope, how will you make it look different from junk mail?
   ★ How you will ensure people look at what you post.
   ★ How you will persuade people to stop speeding.
   ★ Not making your message too complicated. Keep it simple, straightforward and hard-hitting.

PSHE AND CITIZENSHIP 9-11 © MOLLY POTTER 2008

THE POWER OF THE CONSUMER

Some people think carefully about the food they buy and where they buy it from, and some people don't.

Consider these issues:

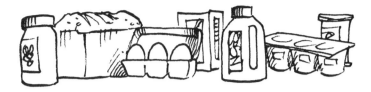

	CONS
FAIR TRADE: some people like to know that the people who grew and farmed the food they buy have been treated well and paid fairly for their work and produce.	
ORGANIC: some people need to know that the food they eat has had no chemicals used to help it grow.	
THE ENVIRONMENT: some people like to buy food that has been grown nearby, so that it is fresh and it has not been transported a very long distance causing lots of pollution when it was transported. These people might also not buy food that has damaged the environment in other ways e.g. rainforest was cut down to grow the crop.	
TYPE OF SHOP: some people buy their food from a shop because it is owned and run by local people and it isn't part of a national chain. This means the money the shop makes remains local.	
COST: some people buy the food they do because it is the cheapest they can find.	
CONVENIENCE: many people just buy food that is most convenient at the time or because the shop they buy it from is close to where they live. Supermarkets are considered convenient because they stock so much and have car parks.	

Think about any disadvantages (cons) to the different types of food buying. Choose from the following and put the appropriate letter into the 'cons' column of the table. More than one letter can go in each box.

A) Not all places stock this type of food.

B) It can be more expensive

C) You might have to look carefully or ask to check the details about this food.

D) It is inconvenient

E) It is not necessarily fair trade

F) The food will not necessarily be organic

G) The environment won't necessarily have been considered during food production and transportation.

I) The profit this food makes will not necessarily remain in the local area.

IF THERE IS TIME...

Design a questionnaire that aims to find out what people think about the issues above.

PSHE AND CITIZENSHIP 9-11 © MOLLY POTTER 2008

CONFLICT

On the island of Jallee there are two types of people: those who believe the sky is more important than the sea (the Jyes) and those who believe the sea is more important than the sky (the Jees).

Every time the Jyes and the Jees get together, they argue about the sea and the sky and they have done this for many years. Because of this conflict, all the Jees now live at one end of the island and the Jyes live at the other. The adult Jyes and Jees spend no time with each other because they are fed up with arguing. The only time when any Jyes and Jees get together is when the children go to the one school on the island.

The Jyes and the Jees hate what has happened and would love someone to come and sort it all out.

Discuss: Which of the following do you think might help sort out the problem on the island of Jallee?

Build a wall between the two sides of the island, build two schools and keep the Jyes and the Jees completely separate.	Get everyone from the island together and discuss the sky and the sea and see if it can be decided for once and for all whether the sky or the sea is best.
Get the Jyes and the Jees together and discuss all their similarities. Talk about what both the Jyes and the Jees would actually want the island to be like.	Encourage the Jyes and the Jees to argue more to try and get them to be so fed up with arguing that they stop.
Make a law and punish the Jyes if they say the sky is better than the sea.	Make a law and punish the Jees if they say the sea is better than the sky.
Encourage the Jyes and the Jees to respect the fact that not everyone believes the same thing. The Jyes and the Jees can start learning this at school.	Try to find out who started the argument and punish that person.